# RACE RELATIONS IN AMERICA

A Christian Guide to Unite
Christians in the Faith

By: Patrick Baldwin

Copyright 2019
American Christian Defense Alliance, Inc.
Baltimore, Maryland
ACDAInc.Org

## Special Request

Thank you for purchasing our book and supporting our Ministry. We actually have two requests – To Pray for Our Ministry and to Read this Book All the Way through. No Ministry can Survive without Prayers and Support so we ask you to keep our Ministry in Your Daily Prayers and Pray as the Lord leads.

We encourage you to Read the Book you purchased all the way through. Many Books NEVER Get Read, and the ones that do only get read the first few pages.

One of our Special Request is that if you are serious about learning the material in this book than you take time to actually read this book, in its entirety – all the way through.

We all lead such busy lives nowadays and can get side tracked so easily, please take a moment to consider my words and read to the end of the book and keep us in Your Prayers.

Thank You once again for purchase. We deeply appreciate Your Prayers and Support and know that God will Bless You as You continue to Bless this Ministry.

Dedication


This book is dedicated to my Brothers and
Sisters in the Lord – Regardless of Your
Race, if You are in Christ You are My
Family and I got Love for You.

# Forward

If you claim that you are not aware of the deep and jagged rift in society called 'racial tension' you are either lying or living in LaLa Land—no disrespect intended. I say this because it is impossible to hear and see the world realistically without knowing that racial tension is a real thing. The mistrust and hostility between people groups is tangible—and sadly, I mean that in the most literal sense of the word.

If this were not true:

- Dylann Roof wouldn't have massacred nine African-American people while they were holding a Bible study / prayer meeting in their church…because of the color of their skin.
- Riots and violence wouldn't have been the norm in Ferguson, MO because the African-American community didn't like the outcome of a court case.
- 9-11 wouldn't have happened.

- Martin Luther King Jr. wouldn't have had a reason to give his famous "I have a dream" speech.
- Rosa Parks wouldn't have made the news for refusing to give up her seat on the bus so that a white man could sit instead of stand.
- The "Knock Out Game" would not exist
- Japanese internment camps wouldn't have indiscriminately locked up all people of Japanese origin as the enemy in the 1940s.
- Millions of Jews wouldn't have been massacred just for being Jewish.
- There would have been one less reason for the Civil War to rip our nation apart.
- The treacherous trek called The Trail of Tears would not have taken place. The grueling hike forced 100,000 Native Americans to leave their homes and settle in government housing. The harsh conditions, utter disrespect for the people, and lack of

provisions resulted in 15,000 deaths along the way.
- General Custer's army would not have knowingly infected hundreds of Native Americans with small pox.
- The murderous hatred between England and Ireland…England and Scotland.
- Jesus' parable of the "Good Samaritan" wouldn't have been necessary.
- The Assyrians, Babylonians, Persians, and Romans wouldn't have kept the Israelites (Jews) under their thumb.
- The Israelites wouldn't have spent 430 years as slaves in Egypt.
- Esau and Ishmael's descendants wouldn't be destined to live in contention with the rest of the world for as long as the world as we know it exists.

This list, though partial, is my way of reminding you that the fact that racial tensions exist in today's society is nothing new. We didn't 'invent' the concept. God did when He destined Ishmael's and Esau's descendants to forever be in contention with everyone else. (Genesis 16 and 27)

The fact that God allowed the 'birth' of hostility between races…even set it into motion…can be confusing. It can even seem contradictory to everything else we know about God—but it isn't. God cannot contradict Himself and He cannot and does not make mistakes. REMEMBER: just because we don't understand something doesn't mean it is wrong. God's treatment of and pronouncements on Ishmael and Esau are a) disciplinary and b) part of God's plan to deal with the sins of the world and of his chosen people. Besides, when it comes right down to it, who can possibly fully know the mind of God? (Romans 11:34) Why would we even try?

The point to be made here is that racial tensions and hostilities exist and always will, because sin exists. But just as it is with every other kind of sin, as Christians we need to resist the sin of racism (which is nothing more than hate) and work to come together as best we can…which brings me to the purpose of this book.

Within the pages of this book you will find Biblical and more modern-day narratives of racial problems along with the lessons we should learn from them; lessons that will make us more like Jesus by loving others as we love ourselves and as Jesus loves us.

We will be starting with one of the earliest incidents of racial hostility and move forward to the world we live in. In doing so, my hope and prayer is that you will use these experiences to inspire and challenge you to do your part in unifying the Body of Christ in Faith through the Blood of Jesus Christ.

# Table of Contents

# Chapter 1: Ham, Ishmael & Esau

**The birth of racial animosity and hatred**

The book of Genesis tells us that it was *Noah*—not Noah and his sons—who found grace in the eyes of the LORD when he (God) totally destroyed all living creatures on the earth and start all over. But because of God's love for Noah and his desire to have additional sources to help repopulate the earth, God also saved Mrs. Noah, along with their sons and daughters in-law.

After getting off the ark, Noah and his sons started farming.  Following the first harvest of his vineyard, however, Noah drank too much of the juice (wine) made from the grapes and got drunk. This in turn led to Ham committing a serious cultural and father/son no nos (which we won't get into here). But because of Ham's actions, in Genesis chapter nine, we read how Noah cursed Ham; telling him that he and his people would be the lowest of low to Shem and Japeth's people (people, being descendants).

We know from the Bible as well as secular history books that Ham's people were and still are the Edomites, Canaanites, Egyptians, Babylonians, Assyrians, Ninevehites, Hitittes, Jebusites, and the people who made up Sodom and Gomorrah (to name a few). So...when Noah cursed Ham, Ham took it to heart. He put it in a petri dish and fed it a steady diet of resentment, anger, and vengefulness; making 'it' grow so fat that it couldn't help but spill over to the next generations, where it is still spilling over even today.

Now I know what some of you are thinking. Some of you are thinking Ham had a right to be angry and that Noah's actions were too harsh. You are thinking that if Noah wouldn't have been in the predicament he was in, Ham wouldn't have done what *he* did. Am I right? Is that what you are thinking?

Well, here's the deal—no one…and I mean absolutely no one can force us to do anything we don't want to do. We ALWAYS have a choice. Even if someone were holding a gun to your head and said do 'this' or die, we would still have a choice. So when Ham *chose* to commit the sin of seeing his father naked, he also *chose* to disrespect and humiliate his father over respecting and honoring him. What's more, once Noah had punished him for his actions, Ham also *chose* to hatred, rebellion, and retaliation over remorsefulness and humility. And as we all know, and as I have already stated, we are still living with the repercussions of Ham's actions and mindset to this very day.

**Moving on to Ishmael**

I'm going to start off by saying I feel sorry for Ishmael. I always have. He was an innocent baby born into a situation he had no control over. He was the victim of Sarah's lack of faith and her jealous insecurity. Ishmael was also the means by which Noah's curse on Ham (which, by the way, was God-approved) would continue to be carried out.

"How?" you ask. I'm so glad you asked...

Genesis 16:1-2 says: *And Sara said unto Abram, Behold now, the Lord hath restrained me from bearing: I pray thee, go in unto my maid; it may be that I may obtain children by her. And Abram hearkened to the voice of Sara.*

Do you see it? Hagar was an *Egyptian* slave; meaning she was a descendant of Ham. So when Sarah realized how foolish she'd been in allowing her slave and her husband to make a baby together, her jealousy turned to all-out prejudice against the boy and his mother. Then in Genesis chapter twenty-one, we see that by the time Isaac finally comes along, Ishmael is prejudiced against Isaac.

This goes a lot deeper than your everyday sibling rivalry. This is deep-seeded hostility and vying for position. But God had a plan all along to make Abraham the father of his (God's) chosen people—the Israelite nation, and He wasn't going to let a not-so-little thing like Sarah's stupidity to stand in the way of things. So he told Abraham to send Hagar and Ishmael away; promising Abraham that Ishmael and his descendants would also become a sizeable nation of people, *but* as the angel of the LORD had told Hagar a few years earlier, Ishmael and his descendants would forever live in hostility toward other nations.

**Fast-forward a few years...**

The Bible tells us in Genesis chapter twenty-five that Isaac and Ishmael came together to bury their father, Abraham. It doesn't say, however, that it was a happy reunion. Why should it have been? The two didn't know each other and Isaac inherited everything Abraham had except for the gifts he gave Ishmael and the children he had with his second wife after Sarah died.

What's more, immediately following the brief text about Isaac and Ishmael burying Abraham, we are once again reminded of the racial hostility that existed between Ishmael's people and everyone else.

As if that weren't enough, Isaac repeats the cycle of dysfunction by joining with his wife, Rebekah, in playing favorites with his twin sons, Jacob and Esau. Rebekah strongly favored Jacob, while Isaac favored Esau. The degree of dysfunction and deceit in this family is unrivaled (past and present). And just as it was with Sarah, God worked around and in spite of Isaac and Rebekah to bring his ultimate plan to fruition in making Jacob (also called Israel) the father of the twelve sons who would become the start of the twelve tribes of Israel.

Why did God choose Jacob over Esau? Why did God even make twins part of the equation? We don't know and quite honestly, it doesn't matter. What *does* matter, though, is that Esau was irresponsible and disrespectful with his position as the oldest son. Esau also refused to own up to his mistakes; choosing instead to rebel and retaliate by adding racial tension and hostility to the dynamics of his already-dysfunctional family by marrying Hittite women. Remember them? The Hittites are descendants of Ham....

Genesis 26:34 says: *When Esau was forty years old, he married Judith daughter of Beeri the Hittite, and also Basemath daughter of Elon the Hittite. They were a source of grief to Isaac and Rebekah. (NIV)*

And so the racial tension continued to grow and spread....

**What this means to you and me**

When God led the Israelites to the Promised Land of Canaan, He gave the Israelites victory over all the idol-worshipping "people" groups, i.e. descendants of Ham, Ishmael, and Esau. We know from looking at a map that these are the countries of Egypt, Turkey, Syria,

Jordan, Iran, Iraq, Israel, and Saudi Arabia today.

Some people may understand from the book of Enoch about fallen angels coming down and breeding with humans and other animals, others may not. This is completely speculation in nature but it stands to reason that God commanded that the Israelites kill every living thing in the promise land because the people and animals in the promise land's DNA was literally contaminated by the fallen angels and their off-spring. On a side note: Remember the last days will be as of the days of Noah (Matt. 24:37/Luke 17:26)

Back now to the topic at hand - We also know that these people are the radical and less-radical Islamic groups, Jews, and a few other lesser-known religions. It goes without saying that there are racial and religious hostilities between us (Americans and even more specifically white Americans) and them as well as between the different sects within their own countries. Sadly, however, this is never going to change this side of heaven.

But what about the rest of the world? Where did those people come from and why are there so many prejudices and hostilities between all of us? Could it be from when God scattered mankind at the tower of Babel?

*But the Lord came down to see the city and the tower which the sons of men had built. And the Lord said, "Indeed the people are one and they all have one language, and this is what they begin to do; now nothing that they propose to do will be withheld from them. Come, let Us go down and there confuse their language, that they may not understand one another's speech." So the Lord scattered them abroad from there over the face of all the earth, and they ceased building the city. Therefore its name is called Babel, because there the Lord confused the language of all the earth; and from there the Lord scattered them abroad over the face of all the earth. ~ Gen. 11:5-9*

The detailed answer to those questions would involve a lot of background data, so I'm going to give it to you in a nutshell:

- The Israelites did not annihilate everyone they went up against as God commended. Those that survived became somewhat nomadic until they came to a place they felt would be suitable in which to make their new home and somewhere they believed they could live in peace.
- The Israelites were scattered when God finally said 'enough is enough'; scattering the ten lost tribes to wherever and the tribes of Judah and Benjamin became scattered throughout the world before Jesus and after Jesus during the persecution of the early Church.

As you let this sink in, think about the conflicts that have happened all over the world since then. Nearly all of them came about because of racial and/or religious intolerance, prejudice, and hostilities because they cannot communicate in a manner that the other can understand – Sound familiar? Each group believes themselves to be superior...right...more deserving...needing to exert their independence...get even for past wrongdoings...or a combination of any or all of these.

The truth of the matter, however, is that until we stop focusing on ourselves and having an attitude of entitlement, being right, and reaching beyond God's laws (and even civil laws) in order to justify our words and our actions, nothing is going to change or get any better. The Bible clearly tells us that Ham's descendants (which include those of Ishmael and Esau) will FOREVER be at odds...at war with everyone else. This fact **is not meant to excuse us or give us permission to participate in racial hostility.**

The fact that these problems will always exist is the **result of sinful rebellion and disobedience against God.** That's it. Plain and simple.

So where does that leave you and me as Christians? It leaves us where we need to be with every other sin. It leaves us with the responsibility to resist the temptations we have to believe and participate in these things. It leaves us with the responsibility to love instead of hate and to set an example for others to do the same.

I'm not saying it is easy. I'm also not saying that love ignores their acts of hatred and violence. We are to stand up for God's people first and foremost. The color of someone's skin, their socio-economic status, their country of origin, or the degree to which they are educated are never reasons to fight. Only when someone is committing acts of evil and are doing things that tries to destroy the things of God or human life are we to stand against them.

Well, that's how it all started. Now it's up to us to keep it at bay and to minimize the instances and affects racial hostility has on our world. Are you up to the task? My prayer is that you are.

# Chapter 2: From Slave to Ruler

Joseph was one of Jacob's sons. He was Jacob's favorite son because he was one of only two sons born to him by his beloved wife Rachel. NOTE: You would have thought Jacob would have learned something about the damage playing favorites among your children can do to a family, but obviously this was not the case.

Anyway...Joseph being the adolescent he was, took it upon himself to 'share' with his brothers the fact that he'd had a dream that was really a vision from God 'saying' that one day his older brother would bow down to him. That, coupled with the fact that Joseph's position as 'favorite son' was so blatantly obvious, led to his brother selling Joseph to some Egyptians (to be a slave). They covered their actions by telling dad, Jacob, that Joseph had been killed by wild animals.

Meanwhile, Joseph ended up in Egypt as one of the household servants for the Pharaoh's right-hand man. While there he was falsely accused of a crime and put in prison. While in prison he once again had the opportunity to use his God-given gift for interpreting dreams. You can read all about it in Genesis chapters thirty-nine and forty.

You can also read in Genesis chapter forty that God was with Joseph in all he did; meaning he blessed Joseph's life and worked through Joseph to do some truly amazing things. Among the amazing things God did by giving Joseph the ability to interpret dreams was to put Joseph in the position of being the most powerful man in all of Egypt—even more so than the Pharaoh, because the Pharaoh trusted Joseph most of all.

So here we have:

- The son of the father of the Israelite nation (or what would grow to be the Israelite nation) sold into slavery

- Working *for* the descendants of Ham
- Rising to a position of authority over the entire nation in spite of the fact that he wasn't 'one of them'
- Working for the good of these people who loved him and put their trust in him because of who he was, rather than looking down on him because he wasn't 'one of them'

This is where things start to get even more interesting…

**People coming together in spite of their differences**

The dreams that Joseph interpreted for Pharaoh enabled Joseph to lead the Egyptians in producing and storing up food over a period of years in preparation for a severe and devastating period of drought and famine (also lasting years).

When this drought and famine actually occurred, the Egyptian people were able to feed everyone in their own land *in addition to* those from other countries who came in search of food. NOTE: It's interesting to me to think about the fact that despite the lack of ability to communicate long-distance and the hardships of traveling, etc., the other nations somehow knew that Egypt was the place to go for food. Somehow they did, though, and Egypt willingly came to their rescue—despite their differences.

Among the many who came for food were Joseph's brothers—the very ones who had sold him into slavery. And who do you think was in charge of doling out the food rations? Yep, Joseph. Now Judah and the rest of the brothers had no idea it was Joseph. After all, they thought he was a slave or possibly even dead. They certainly didn't have any reason to think he was the top-dog in all of Egypt. But Joseph recognized them.

Because Joseph's heart was so in tune to God's and because Joseph had the wisdom to realize that his brothers' actions were really a blessing and part of God's plan for his life, Joseph had no animosity toward them. He was happy to see them. He wanted to know how his dad was...how his little brother (who wasn't with them) was. Joseph played it cool, though. He didn't reveal himself to them on their first visit. Instead, he concocted a scenario that required a few more visits before finally revealing his identity (Genesis 45). It's one of the most beautiful accounts in history recorded for us in the Bible.

Because of Joseph's status in Egypt, once the Pharaoh learned that Joseph's family had been there, he told Joseph to bring them all there to live. So they did. They settled in the Land of Goshen.

Throughout these years of caring for others, racial tensions do not appear to have been an issue. It wasn't until after Joseph and the Pharaoh he served under died that things began to take a turn for the worse.

**Racial inequality**

The first chapter of Exodus tells us that the Israelites had a bit of a population explosion—so much so that the Pharaoh (who again, didn't care anything about what Joseph had done to avoid a world-crisis) started worrying about the possibility of 'those people' getting to secure in their position in his country. Enter: racial hostility and discrimination.

The Pharaoh forced the Israelites into slavery; treating them with severe cruelty. This remained their lot in life for four hundred years.

During this time they were beaten, oppressed, made to work under grueling and near-impossible conditions. Just because they were 'different'? Just because they weren't Egyptians? Well, yes and no. On the surface or to the human eye, those were the reasons for the Israelites being enslaved. Beyond that, however, was the fact that this was God's doing.

God told Abraham back in the fifteenth chapter of Genesis that the Israelites would be enslaved for four hundred years. Why?

The answer to that is one only God can give us for sure, but most likely it was to teach them humility, empathy, perseverance, and to provide a stark contrast to what he was going to do for them in making them his chosen people. The reasons really aren't all that important. What matters is that we learn from this period in history so that we Christians don't repeat it.

**What this means to you and me**

There are actually several racially-related lessons to be learned from Joseph's life. Let's look at a few of them (in no order of relevance or importance.

LESSON #1: You should choose your friends and associates based on who they are on the inside—not what they look like or what you *think* they can 'bring to the table'.

If Pharaoh and his officials wouldn't have been willing to look beyond Joseph's ethnicity, the known world would have suffered greatly. Countless people would have starved to death.

When you meet new people, hire a new employee, get new neighbors, or anything else that requires you to interact with someone you don't already know, how do you decide which people to date, hang out with, hire, extend a hardy welcome to, or...?

When you hear or see a news report about an act of violence or incident involving people of different races, ethnic groups or religions, do you make automatic assumptions as to who is right or innocent based on their color, their demeanor, or their socio-economic status.

As Christians we shouldn't make snap-judgements based on appearances. We should judge the situation based on facts. We should take the time to look beyond the surface to the heart of the situation. And if we don't have immediate access to those things, we need to either get them in order to make an informed decision or remove ourselves from the situation.

LESSON #2: Humility and mercy serve to benefit you and everyone around you.

Joseph could have used his power in a lot of ways. He could have been self-serving, retaliatory, and vengeful. But he didn't. He humbled himself to be God's servant no matter what God asked of him. He didn't use his position as a means to get back at his brothers for what they did to him. Instead, he chose to forgive them and see the big picture and the good that came from it.

As Christians we cannot give into the temptation to seek revenge on those who wrong us. We have been called to love as Jesus loves; not seeing skin color or other dividing issues.

As Christians we need to remember that in God's eyes we are all equally valuable, equally worthy of his love, and equally worthy to be respected and accepted by our fellow man.

LESSON #3: Fear of what we don't understand is a dangerous thing.

The new pharaoh didn't know Joseph. Didn't care what Joseph had done. Didn't want to take the time to learn how or why the Israelites were in his country. He didn't try to form a cohesive bond with them that would have served to make Egypt even stronger. No, he just got scared because 'those people' were different than him. They weren't Egyptians, so they couldn't have much to offer. They needed to be put in their place before they got any 'funny' ideas.

Over the years, how many times have you avoided people or situations because they were different than what you were used to? How many different races of people attend your church? How segregated is your community? Would you be scared or uneasy if you found yourself to be the minority in a restaurant, store, or other public gathering place?

As Christians we need to see ourselves and others as fellow-human beings and fellow-creations of our heavenly Father. If you refuse to see color your color-blindness will eventually catch on. And when that happens, something else happens—peace, community, and unity among the races.

Open-mindedness, humility, and seeing people for who they are—not what they are…*this* is how God wants us to treat one another.

# Chapter 3: Perspective

The Old Testament book of Esther is the account of how a humble, beautiful Jewish girl named Esther became the queen of the Persian Empire and used her position to save the entire Jewish race. It is beautiful story. But the role Esther plays is only half the story. The *reason* Esther has to use her position to save her people and how she finds the courage to do so is where the rest of the story is found and the part of the story we are going to focus on now. Mordecai and Haman's relationship is what we are going to focus on because their relationship is where the lessons in how (and how not to) deal with racial prejudices can be found.

The racial tensions between Mordecai and Haman boil over when pride and arrogance clash with faithfulness to God, with a little dose of skepticism and worry thrown in for good measure.

## Skepticism and worry

Mordecai is the guilty party when it comes to feeling worried and skeptical. So when Esther was summoned to the palace to compete for the honor of being queen, Mordecai warned Esther against talking about her ethnicity. Not bothering to mention (hiding) the fact that she was Jewish was for her own good, he told her.

Honestly, though, you can't fault Mordecai for feeling this way. After all, the Jewish people were living as a captive people. They were part of the spoils of war when the Persian Empire conquered the Babylonians, who had beat out the Assyrians, who had initially taken the Israelite people captive.

The mindset of skepticism and worry stuck with Esther. We see this to be true when Mordecai decided it was time for Esther to use her Jewish heritage to save the entire nation from being assassinated by the Persian army because of false accusations against them.

At first Esther refused. Doing so put her life at risk and she wasn't sure she could do it...or if she even wanted to.

Romans 1:16 says: *For I am not ashamed of the gospel of Christ: for it is the power of God unto salvation to everyone that believeth; to the Jew first, and also to the Greek.* As Christians we cannot be ashamed or afraid to be known and recognized as a Christian. Likewise, we should give others the grace to display and live their heritage without fear of being made fun of or discriminated against.

**Pride and arrogance vs. faith**

The deeper racial rift was made when Mordecai refused to bow down to the arrogant and prideful Haman (King Xerxes' right-hand man). Mordecai's refusal to bow down to anyone other than God infuriated Haman so much that he tricked  King Xerxes into issuing a law to have every Jew killed...murdered for no other reason than the fact that they were Jewish.

Sound familiar? Haman's prejudices were nothing more than a bruised ego gone wild.

Mordecai was undoubtedly right in refusing to bow down to Haman. Again, tolerance toward people should never go against God's commands and expectations for his people. But there is ALWAYS a way to love and accept people where they are *so that* we can love them to where they need to be...in the family of God.

**What this means to you and me**

Haman's vengeful heart has been seen in others over the centuries and can still be seen in people even still today. Hopefully, however, your heart will never be one of them.

Don't let pride and arrogance taint your thoughts and feelings toward others just because they don't happen to be like you.

Don't adopt false feelings of superiority because you were 'there first' or are in the majority.

Instead, try to win them to the LORD through the bold exercise of your faith in action - by sharing the truth of the Gospel of Jesus Christ with them in love and sincerity, not wanting any of them to burn in hell.

# Chapter 4: Not Our Call

How many times have you heard (or said) something along the lines of:

"Trying to help 'those people' is a complete waste of time."

"'They' don't want to better their situation—they would rather keep on blaming everyone else for their situation."

"You can't help someone who doesn't want help."

"'They' don't think they are doing anything wrong, so whatever we say or do won't matter."

"Hating and blaming everyone but themselves for their problems is a way of life for 'them' and they don't want that to change."

Jonah could have said (and probably did say) all of the above when God told him to go to Nineveh. Jonah believed going to

Nineveh was a complete waste of time and energy. The people of Nineveh, who were descendants of Ham, by the way, were a godless and rambunctious people. In Jonah's mind there was no way they would listen. There was no reason for him to waste his time and risk his life by going to Nineveh. 'Those people' weren't worth the effort! They were…a lost cause.

Jonah's prejudices were intense. He was so dead-set against lowering himself to associate with those troublemakers that he tried running away from God and the job God had given him to do.

That was Jonah's first mistake; thinking he could make the call on who was a lost cause and who wasn't. It didn't take him long to figure out that in fact it wasn't his call and that he was going to Nineveh whether he wanted to or not. To his credit, Jonah didn't argue with or try to outwit God a second time. He went, did what he was supposed to do, and much to his surprise, the Ninevehites actually listened! The king ordered the people to repent and call on God to forgive them.

You would think Jonah would have been happy to have played such an important part in saving an entire nation from God's wrath of destruction, but he wasn't. When you read the last chapter of the book of Jonah it is obvious that Jonah is not pleased with the way things turned out. It's like he wanted to be able to give God a great big "I told you so", but couldn't. So instead, he basically tells God that what he did wasn't fair or a very good idea. Jonah's prejudice is still so deeply planted in his heart and mind that he didn't want the Ninevehites to have a chance to know God.

God quickly reminds Jonah that it's not his call. From there God goes on to say that it is up to Him to decide who is spared and who isn't. None of us is more worthy in God's eyes because He created each of us. He loves us all with an equal amount of love. He desires that each of us come to know

Him personally and passionately with the same amount of desire in his heart.

Did the Ninevehites remain repentant and focused on God? No, they did not. History (both in the Bible and secularly) reveal that Nineveh, which is buried under modern-day Mosul, Iraq, was a culturally diverse and progressive city that valued intellect and the arts, but had no desire to know and experience the deity and holiness of God.

Do these facts about Nineveh and its short-lived repentance make Jonah justified in his thoughts and actions? Absolutely not. 'Lost causes' are not our call.

**What does this mean to you and me**

I think Jonah's situation and the handling of it are especially relevant to each of us in today's society. Why? Because if we are being honest with ourselves most of us would have to admit that when it comes to certain groups of people we act very similarly to Jonah.

The Bible *does* say that there will be hostility between us and the rest of the world – We shall be hated in all the world for Christ's name sake according to the Bible. However, we have to look past race and color to the Blood of Jesus Christ that units us in one faith and one family – The family of God.

BUT...there are still a couple of things we need to learn from the book of Jonah when it comes to our way of thinking and handling situations with people we believe to be lost causes.

We need to learn that **it isn't up to us to decide who has a right to hear and possibly accept Jesus Christ as their Lord and Savior.** Jesus' last words before returning to heaven were instructions to each of us to go and make disciples. So whoever is in your section of the world that is who you need to be showing and telling about Jesus.

You can't make them want to listen and obey, but equally true is the fact that you don't have the right or the power to decide if they get the chance to do so.

We also need to learn that **success cannot and should not be measured in numbers.** The shepherd in Jesus' parable left ninety-nine sheep to look for one. The angels rejoice over one lost soul who is saved. In spite of the fact that Jesus healed ten lepers, only one took hold of the spiritual healing that was offered too; something that wouldn't have happened had Jesus not taken the time to care for this seemingly lost cause group of men.

Our job is *not* to decide who deserves to hear or who is worth the effort and the risk. These things have already been decided for us by God. He says everyone deserves and that everyone is worth the effort and the risk. Our job is to show and tell the world around us who Jesus is. Are you ready, willing, and able to do your job?

# Chapter 5: BEWARE

The Old Testament of the Bible focuses on the establishment, glory days, fall, and promised re-establishment of the nation of Israel. The setting of the Old Testament is wide-spread. It covers most, if not all, of the inhabited world in those days and times. The events recorded naturally lend themselves to contact and conflict with other people groups and provide valuable information and teaching on how we as Christians should handle ourselves when it comes to loving those who are different from us and drawing the lines in the sand.

The New Testament, however, focuses on two things: Jesus the Messiah and Savior of all man and the establishment of the Church. In New Testament times there are still numerous different nationalities and different sects of people, but now they have been condensed down into three major distinctions: Jew, Samaritan, or Gentile.

Jews were those who were direct descendants of Judah or Benjamin (the two remaining tribes of Israel). Gentiles were anyone from another specific and distinct nationality. Samaritans were biracial people; people who were descendants of Israelites who had married into the pagan people groups we read about in the Old Testament—the people groups God demanded the Israelites NOT to marry.

## Jews vs. Gentiles

The tensions between the Jews and the Gentiles were, for the most part, purely based on religious differences and feelings of superiority. The Jews enjoyed riding on the proverbial coattails of their ancestors as God's chosen people. They believed the prophets who said a Messiah was coming who would re-establish the kingdom and restore them to a place of honor. The problems with this was:

- They allowed their hope to make them arrogant and prideful. The fact that they were under the oppressive rule of the Roman Empire, they had a "just-wait-till-our-Messiah"-gets-here attitude. It was all about being number one again in their minds.

- They completely missed the part about being humble before God. The Jewish leaders (Pharisees, Sadducees...) were more interested in man -instituted rituals and maintaining their power over the Jewish people than they were leading the people toward a life of reverent fear, faith, and obedience to God.

They looked down on the Gentiles because they considered them dirty and in a constant state of defilement because of the foods they ate, the fact that they didn't circumcise their baby boys, and several other matters of the Law of Moses. Oh, and of course many of the Gentile people were polytheistic, so that was another reason to hate them.

The Gentiles, on the other hand, looked at the Jews as arrogant, pompous, and a bunch of wanna-be dreamers.

The barriers were in place and the racial tensions ran deep; something that wouldn't be easy for either group to get over once God decided it was time for this to happen.

**Stay away from those Samaritans**

The Samaritans were the misfits of society. They weren't really Jewish. They weren't really Gentiles. They were a biracial group of people no one wanted to claim.

To the Jews the Samaritans were a reminder of the disobedience of their ancestors. God specifically *commanded* the Israelites (Jews) NOT to marry people who were not also Israelites. God knew this would not work. He knew that if they intermarried they would not remain true to Him and would begin to incorporate the worship practices of their pagan spouses into their own worship.

The Israelites, didn't listen or obey God - they married pagan men and women and left God to worship idols. We also know that God's patience ran out—thus the reason they were living under the oppression of the Roman Empire. But the presence and reality of God wasn't completely lost in these relationships, however, because thousands of years later we see that the Samaritan people knew of God, believed in God, and even hoped for God. We see this in the conversation Jesus had with the Samaritan woman about the living water of salvation through Him…

*The woman said unto Him, Sir, I perceive that thou art a prophet. Our fathers worshipped in this mountain; and the Jews say, that in Jerusalem is the place where men ought to worship. Jesus said unto her, Woman, believe me, the hour comes, when you shall neither in this mountain, nor in Jerusalem, worship the Father. You worship what you know not: we know who we worship: for salvation is of the Jews. But the hour comes, and now is, when the true worshippers shall worship the Father in spirit and in truth: for the Father seeks such to worship Him. God is a Spirit: and they that worship Him must worship Him in spirit and in truth. The woman said unto Him, I know that Messiah comes, which is called Christ: when He is come, He will tell us all things. Jesus said unto her, I that speak unto thee am He. And upon this came his disciples, and marveled that he talked with the woman: yet no man said, What seekest thou? or, Why talkest thou with her? (John 4:19-27)*

The Israelites started the whole 'Samaritan thing', but by the time the Jews of the New Testament came onto the scene, they didn't want to own their part in things. They wanted to sweep that part of their history under the rug; pretending it wasn't there.

And if treating the Samaritans like scum was involved…so be it.

**Moving on to the lepers**

Of all the prejudices we will talk about, this one is the most justifiable. And here's why I say this: The Law of Moses commanded that people with leprosy and other diseases be removed from the general population as a means of containing the disease or illness. The lack of medical skill and knowledge made it necessary—the smart thing to do.

What I'm trying to say is that it wasn't the fact that they separated these folks from everyone else that was bad. It was their treatment of them that made things less than they should have been.

I get it—they were scared of the possibilities and of the unknown. But being scared doesn't have to or shouldn't translate into rudeness.

**What does this mean to you and me**

We're going to work backwards on this one by starting with the prejudices and tensions brought on by fear or intimidation of the unknown and those things that simply make us uncomfortable....

A young mother whose son is adopted from an Asian country was told by one of his four year-old peers that he wasn't receiving an invitation to his birthday party because his mom (the birthday boy's) didn't know the language the adopted boy spoke.

First of all, Silas speaks English. Yes, it isn't always very clear and yes, he does have a few speech impediments. But for the love of ice cream, what does that matter? And what does it matter that the birthday boy's mom might not be able to understand every word he says? This is a classic case of prejudice because of ignorant fear or intimidation.

Equally in need of fixing are the incidents where adults shun people *and* direct their kids in shunning people in wheelchairs, people with scarred faces or bodies, people covered in tattoos, who have weird hairdos, or who have obvious disabilities such as turrets, ADHD, or Down's.

Not Cool!

Whether you are willing to admit it or not, you aren't any more perfect than these people are. Your imperfections are just less obvious. So they have special needs—that doesn't make them bad or less. It just means they have special needs.

I get that often times your feelings and actions aren't the result of actual prejudice, but rather stem from uncertainty of knowing how to respond or interact. I also know that often times a parent's act of pulling their child away comes from a desire to not have them ask or say something inappropriate or embarrassing to either party. But again, don't go there. Instead, give your child the opportunity to know and be blessed by those who are different from them. Give those with special needs the blessing of being seen for who they are—not what they can or cannot do. Give yourself the privilege of being able to know you are seeing others as God sees them.

Now let's move on to the matter of dealing with racial and ethnic tensions because of race and religion. Let me drop a few basic facts and then provide you with the Biblical examples we are to follow.

Fact #1: Someone's color or cultural background is not a determining factor of their worth to society. The things that determine one's worth to society are:

- Our Christian witness and character—is it genuine and sincere
- Our integrity, which is our moral character and our treatment of others (love, respect, honesty, compassion, kindness)
- Our willingness to obey the law
- Our sense of responsibility and loyalty to our country

- Our sense of responsibility to work hard and provide for our own needs

Fact #2: The fact that someone looks or thinks, differently than we do doesn't make them bad or less. The only thing we need to concern ourselves with here is that we do whatever we can to share the great news of the Gospel with everyone we can in a way that brings honor and glory to God.

The racial and cultural divides our world has experienced over the last four hundred years or so have been devastating, to say the least. But not all divisions are bad. Some are born out of the need to keep the Church healthy and growing. Remember, it was because of a division over religious beliefs and the refusal to accept the norm being forced upon believers that laid the groundwork for the United States of America to even exist. Similarly, Jesus and his followers broke away from the traditions of the Law to fulfill God's ultimate plan. But in each of these instances, it wasn't about one group of people believing they were superior to another. In each of these instances it was about a group of people choosing God's ways over man's ways.

The same can be said about Peter. Peter took a tremendous risk when he boldly walked through the racial barriers of prejudice between the Jews and the Gentiles. When Peter unashamedly and obediently preached the message of the Gospel to Cornelius and his family and then to countless other Gentiles, he was wiping out centuries of prejudice.

And let's not forget Paul. Paul traveled throughout Greece, Asia, Italy, and the Mideast sharing the Gospel with countless people from all different nationalities, socio-economic backgrounds, and beliefs. No one was too far gone or too lost to hear the Word being preached.

How much like Jesus are you?

## Chapter 6: Civil War?

There Was Nothing Civil About the Civil War

In the minds of most people, the Civil War was all about slavery—whether it was right or wrong. But the truth of the matter is that the issue of slavery was only one reason the Civil War was fought. The primary and reason for this awful war was state's rights. The southern states believed their interests would be better served (including their interest in slavery) if they could govern themselves independently of the United States government. In other words, they wanted to leave the union that is our country. The north, on the other hand, said no way! They said that the country could not be dismantled. They also said that slavery should be abolished and that people had a right to be free citizens regardless of the color of their skin. But just because they believed slavery was wrong and that black people had the right to be free didn't mean the North wasn't without its share of prejudice.

There were a few northern states where slavery was accepted and practiced—Delaware, North Carolina, and Maryland were the three northern states with slaves during the 1860s. Black men were drafted into the Union army, but were not usually allowed to fight with white men. What's more, they were paid significantly less than their peers who were white.

As far as the Southern states go, less than twenty-five percent of the population in the South actually owned slaves. But that less-than-twenty-five-percent owned between three and four million slaves. The point to be made here is this: countless soldiers fighting for the South during the Civil War weren't fighting to preserve slavery. It meant nothing to them. The majority were fighting out of a sense of pride for their state, their belief in state's rights, and/or a sense of duty and loyalty to the place they called home.

Regardless of the actual reasons for the war's onset, the fact remains that the issue of slavery played a major role in the whole sordid affair. What you might not know, however, is that the Emancipation Proclamation signed into law by President Abraham Lincoln on January 1, 1863 didn't put an end to slavery across the board. The Emancipation Proclamation granted freedom to only those three to four million slaves in the rebellious southern states. Granted, that's a lot of people who had their freedom granted to them, but it wasn't all-inclusive. Those slaves outside the Confederacy (including those in Union states) were not granted their freedom legally until the 13th Amendment was added to the Constitution in December of 1865.

Okay, so now that you've had your history lesson for the week, let's talk about what this has to do with current-day America and what it means to you and me.

**What this means to you and me**

The lessons I want us to learn from the Civil War are as follows:

LESSON #1: No one has the right to own another person. No dollar value can or should be placed on a human life. We were all purchased by the blood of Jesus Christ for the purpose of being redeemed so that we can spend eternity in God's presence if we so choose. One price paid was for all on that Good Friday and we will never be 'for sale' again.

LESSON #2: Prejudice and racial hostilities don't stop until there is a change of heart.

Just because a piece of paper said a man, woman, or child was no longer a slave didn't automatically guarantee they wouldn't be treated as such.

Just because the Union said black people shouldn't be slaves didn't mean they believed them to be their equals in all things.

Just because as person was a slave didn't always mean they were abused and lived in constant fear and dread for their lives.

Just because a slave was granted their freedom didn't automatically mean their life took a 360. Many chose to remain where they were for pay or went to work (for pay) doing the very same jobs they had done for their 'masters' for someone else.

The only thing that can remove prejudice and racial hostility from a society is a change of heart – Meaning a Spiritual Revival the Sweeps Across the Land. People have to think and feel differently about their fellow man before they can begin to see them and treat them as equals – and the only way to do that is through the eyes of God.

We've come a long way since the days of slavery in our nation, but we still have a long way to go so let's continue to pray for revival in our nation.

# Chapter 7: Genocide & Democide

Democide is nothing more than the Killing of People by their Government. Every single time this started with labeling others inferior or less than human in some way. This of course led to prejudices and racism – which at its core in nothing more than hatred. It should be noted here that prior to Democide the government always disarms or attempts to disarm the general population (especially those who are the political or cultural opposition).

The Jewish Holocaust is possibly the most talked about act of Democide today. However, both Communist Russia and China had killed much greater numbers of their populations then Fascist Germany. Yet let's look at Germany since more people are probably more familiar with the dynamics.

The Holocaust And Beyond

The Holocaust was undoubtedly one of the most horrific event in modern history. The word 'modern' even seems to be an incorrect word to use. What is modern about the senseless annihilation of millions of people just because of their physical appearance and their religious convictions? How could anyone possibly justify their murders and those of anyone caught trying to protect them? Even the various empires that ruled over Israel were more tolerant and merciful of the Israelites' religious beliefs. It was, in the minds of most, nothing short of insanity allowed to morph into pure evil.

The Holocaust, which was the near-extinction of the world's population of Jewish people, resulted in the deaths of MILLIONS (approximately eleven) of people—the majority of which were Jews. The rest were Gentiles (Christians and those who just recognized the wrong of it all) who dared to try to protect their friends and neighbors.

We know why these people died. They died because they were Jewish. But what we don't often stop to think about is why Hitler's hatred for the Jewish race drove him to commit countless acts of pure evil. And truthfully, it is only by knowing why he harbored such a deep-seeded hatred and prejudice toward the Jewish population that we will be able to prevent something like this from happening again.

Scholars, theologians, and humanitarians across the globe would agree that in many ways we learned some hard lessons from the Holocaust. But when I look at some of the things going on in the world today, I have to wonder just how good of a student society has been.

**Religious persecution still exists**

Reports from various sources say that approximately one hundred thousand

Christians are killed each year *because of* their faith /religious beliefs. This is religious persecution. See we have enough external threats to worry about without being divided over our race or cultural backgrounds as Christians. We need to unit and stand together. Think about it for a minute, what other religion is being persecuted like Christians are?

The same cannot be said about those practicing other world religions (Muslims, Buddhists, Atheists, Scientologists...). Why? Because the Bible tells us that we will be hated in all the world for Christ's name sake. The world hated Christ and wanted to destroy Him . . . but He rose again on the third day and now we have the victory over the enemy. Let us not turn on one another and devour one another – Remember a house divided cannot stand.

Let's look at America right now - More and more school districts have banned the singing or playing of religious Christmas carols in their holiday programs.

Children and teenagers have been sent home from school to change clothes because their shirt has a Bible verse or other Christian religious message on it.

Many school districts across the country have banned Bibles from being read on school property—even during free reading time.

All of these are forms of religious persecution aimed at Christians. They result from the complaints and actions taken by other religions and non-believers in the 'name' of equal rights. But where are the rights of Christians in all of this?

**Blame leads to hate and racial hostility**

I want to go back to a question I posed a few paragraphs ago—the one that asked why Hitler hated Jews. The answer to that question can pretty much be summed up like this: Hitler blamed the German Jewish population's indifference to WWI for Germany losing that war. His resentment of them and his passionate belief in his country's superiority blossomed into hate and the hate into what we call the Holocaust.

The Holocaust is one of the most blatant example of what blaming someone else can lead to, but it's not the first time this has happened, and unfortunately it will not be the last.

**Prejudice is ignorance**

The official definition of the word prejudice is: "preconceived opinion that is not based on reason or actual experience"

I don't know about you, but in my opinion, that's the same as ignorance.

The Holocaust stemmed from prejudice (ignorance) about why Germany lost WWI.

The prejudice that believed that all Japanese people in the United States were possible spies for the county of Japan during WWII was ignorance toward the loyalties and convictions of individuals.

Prejudice that bullies its way into the schools, our communities, and even the clothes we wear, and the principles by which we run our privately-owned businesses is ignorance toward what Christianity really is and toward the boundaries of where one person's rights overlaps another's.

**What does this mean to you and me?**

When we look at the events that led to the Holocaust and those that have taken place since then (and are still taking place), we need to remember:

- It is never okay to assume we know why a person feels or thinks the way they do or even that they feel or think the way we *believe* they do.
- It is never okay to believe mental, emotional, or physical violence is the means by which we should try to win people over.
- When we feel prejudices creeping into our heart and mind (and they

will) we need to take the time to learn so we can discern instead of assuming in ignorance.

Most importantly, however, we need to be prepared and willing to suffer for the cause of Christ. We need to be unashamed of the Gospel and of who we are as Christians. Scary? Yes. Desirable? Not really. Worth it? Always and forever.

*For I am not ashamed of the gospel of Christ: for it is the power of God unto salvation to everyone that believeth; to the Jew first, and also to the Greek. (Romans 16:1)*

*Blessed are ye, when men shall revile you, and persecute you, and shall say all manner of evil against you falsely, for my sake. Rejoice, and be exceeding glad: for great is your reward in heaven: for so persecuted they the prophets which were before you. (Matthew 5:11-12)*

# Chapter 8: The Dream

If you are under the age of fifty you have little to no idea what the Civil Rights Movement really meant to society. You don't know, because you haven't lived in a society where black people weren't allowed to attend the same schools, drink out of the same water fountains, sit wherever they wanted to in a restaurant or movie theater like white people. You didn't see news reports about lynch mobs and KKK rallies being presented matter-of-factly. Praise God, you didn't grow up this way.

Moving forward even a few more years...thankfully today most of us aren't raising our children to believe they can catch AIDS by being in the same room with or being friends with someone who has this disease and we aren't refusing to let our children have friends who look or speak differently than we do.

We've come a long way over the past fifty years, but we've still got a long way to go. If that weren't true we wouldn't turn on the news to see angry, hate-filled eyes and hear angry, hate-filled voices claiming discrimination.

If this weren't true we wouldn't be hearing and seeing news of bombings and mass-shootings by people claiming to be doing these things in the name of Allah or to bring 'death to America'.

**What does this mean to you and me?**

Rather than repeat a lot of what I've already said—I want to end this chapter by sharing with you a portion of Martin Luther King Jr's. "I Have A Dream" speech.

Martin Luther King, Jr. had black skin, but he didn't want to be recognized as a black man. He wanted to be recognized as a man. Period. He wanted people to look past the outward appearance and into the heart and mind of individuals. He wanted people to be valued and respected for the fact that they

were human beings. Period. Yet he. didn't
come up with that on his own. He was
simply relaying the message of the Gospel.
We have been called to do the same.

*...I have a dream that my four little children
will one day live in a nation where they will
not be judged by the color of their skin but
by the content of their character...*

*...And when this happens, when we allow
freedom to ring, when we let it ring from
every village and every hamlet, from every
state and every city, we will be able to
speed up that day when all of God's
children, black men and white men, Jews
and Gentiles, Protestants and Catholics, will
be able to join hands and sing in the words
of the old Negro spiritual, "Free at last! free
at last! thank God Almighty, we are free at
last!"*

# Chapter 9: One More Look Back

I hope you've not missed the fact that this book is laid out in a chronological order of sorts; starting with Ham and going to near-current times. I do, however, want to take one more trip back in time—wayyyy back in time to the days of the early Church. Specifically, to the New Testament book of Philemon.

The book of Philemon is one of the shortest books in the Bible. It is only one chapter long and that one chapter has only twenty-five verses. But within those twenty-five verses is a powerful message about racial hostility and prejudice.

In a nutshell, here is what the book of Philemon is about:

- Paul wrote this letter to Philemon in an effort to persuade Philemon to accept his former slave, Onesimus as a brother in Christ rather than to see him only as a slave.

- It seems that Onesiumus had run away after stealing from Philemon. But while on the run, Onesimus met Paul and was introduced to the truth of the Gospel.
- Paul was sending Onesimus back to Philemon—not as a slave, but as a brother in Christ.
- Paul was so convinced of Onesimus' sincere faith and transformation of character that he told Philemon that whatever Onesimus owed him (Philemon), Paul would cover.
- Paul reminded Philemon that it was his Christian duty to forgive and move forward without any prejudice against Onesimus.

Paul was good at being able to look deeper than someone's appearance and to not judge them based on their prior activities or on the actions of their family, friends, or the belief system and character of 'their people' in general. Paul was good at this because he had once been a Pharisee of Pharisees; a man guilty of murdering Christians and enjoying it. Paul knew people could be changed by the power of the Gospel because he was one of them.

**What does this mean to you and me?**

The message I want you to get from Paul's letter to Philemon is short and sweet—just like the letter itself. The message is this: God can change anyone's heart that allows him to do so. None of us are above needing salvation and none of us are below or too far gone to receive it. SO...none of us should ever feel we have the right to decide who we accept into the family of God based on what they look like, where they come from, the amount of money they have, the clothes they wear, or the way they talk. The only requirement for being part of God's family, is this:

- *Then Peter said unto them, Repent, and be baptized every one of you in the name of Jesus Christ for the remission of sins, and ye shall receive the gift of the Holy Ghost. (Acts 2:38)*

- *Jesus said unto him, Thou shalt love the Lord thy God with all thy heart, and with all thy soul, and with all thy mind. This is the first and great commandment.  And the second is like unto it, Thou shalt love thy neighbor as thyself.(Matthew 22:37-39)*

# Chapter 10: Think About It

As we close I want to give you a list of quotes that are meant to encourage you to put prejudice and racial hostility far from you, teach you to discern between prejudice your Christian duty, and prick your heart and your conscience so that you are never guilty of treating your fellow man in a way that displeases and dishonors God

Remember—there is more than one kind of prejudice and more than one kind of slavery. Let's get rid of them all.

**Quotes**

- *Racism isn't born, folks, it's taught. I have a two-year-old son. You know what he hates? Naps! End of list. ~Dennis Leary*

- *To live anywhere in the world today and be against equality because of race or color is like living in Alaska and being against snow. ~William*

*Faulkner, Essays, Speeches and Public Letters*

- *Laundry is the only thing that should be separated by color. ~Author unknown*

- *Racial superiority is a mere pigment of the imagination. ~Author Unknown*

- *Racism is man's gravest threat to man - the maximum of hatred for a minimum of reason. ~Abraham Joshua Heschel*

- *There is More that Unites Us then Divides Us – Unknown Author*

- *The Two Greatest Commandments are to Love the Lord Your God with all Your Heart, with all Soul and with all Your Mind and to Love Your Neighbor as Yourself – Jesus Christ.*

A House Divide Cannot Stand -God

## Special Gift

God has a Gift for You!   The Plan of
Salvation:

There is no formal prayer of salvation as
many churches would have you believe,
God's Word is very clear - there is only one
way to get to the Father in heaven and that
is through Jesus Christ (John 14:6). Jesus
says that you must be born again to enter
into heaven (John 3:3-5).

Salvation is simply the first step in building
an open and honest relationship with God.
We all have sinned and fallen short, but
there is Hope in Jesus Christ - Just cry out to
God in sincerity and honesty asking for
forgiveness and for Him to Save you,
Sanctify you, and fill you with His Holy Spirit
- Ask for His will to be done in your life on
earth as it is in Heaven and That's it, now
just keep it real with God.

A Warning:

The Christian walk is not an easy life on the surface. The Word of God says that we will be hated in all the world for Christ namesake (Matt. 24:9).  The Bible says that in the last days are enemy prevail against us physically until Christ returns to save us (Dan 7:21, 22). Furthermore, we must endure hardship as a good soldier of Jesus Christ (2 Tim 2:3) and yet we are never alone in this, God promises us that He will never leave us nor forsake us if we believe in him (Matt.28:20).

In everything we go through we have the peace and joy of God which surpasses all understanding (Philp. 4:6-8) The Bible declares, "For I consider the sufferings of this present time are not worthy to be compared with the glory which shall be revealed in us". (Rom 8:18). However, in all these things we are more than conquerors through Jesus Christ (Rom. 8:37)

# Stay in Contact

Stay in Contact with the American Christian Defense Alliance, Inc. through Our Website At: ACDAInc.Org


Join Our Mailing List

We also Greatly Appreciate You Signing Up for Our Mailing List and Providing a Good Rating and review for this Book. Your reviews help other people like yourself find this book on Amazon and benefit from its contents.


If You or Your Family have been Blessed by this book please let us know by dropping us a line through our website at ACDAInc.Org

# Find All Our Books

<u>Some of Our Books:</u>

Parenting: How to Be A Great Parent And Raise Awesome Kids

Parenting Economics 101: How to be Financially Stable in an Unstable World

Wisdom from Your Elders: Learning From Your Parents, Grandparents, and the Older People in Your Church

Salvation for Your Unsaved Mom: 10 Things to Tell Your Mom Before She Dies

Parenting Special Needs Children: A Christian Guide to Parenting Children with ADHD, Autism, Asperger's, and other Psychological, Behavioral, or Physiological Disorders

Additional Formats

Thank you for reading this book. Your support and the support of others continue to humble us and enable our Ministry to grow. We hope and pray that this book has blessed you in some way. If you enjoyed this book consider purchasing it in additional formats or giving it as a gift to someone who could benefit from it.

We have this book available as an E-Book, Paperback, and Audio Book. We have no way to know which format you purchased our book in but want to make you aware that this book can be found in multiple formats. So please consider purchasing our book in additional formats to further support our Ministry or Bless someone Special in your life.

We Greatly Appreciate Your Support as Well as You Sharing this information, including links to our books with Others on Your Social Media Platforms

Thank You Once Again for Your Support; We
Know God Will Bless You as You Have
Blessed This Ministry